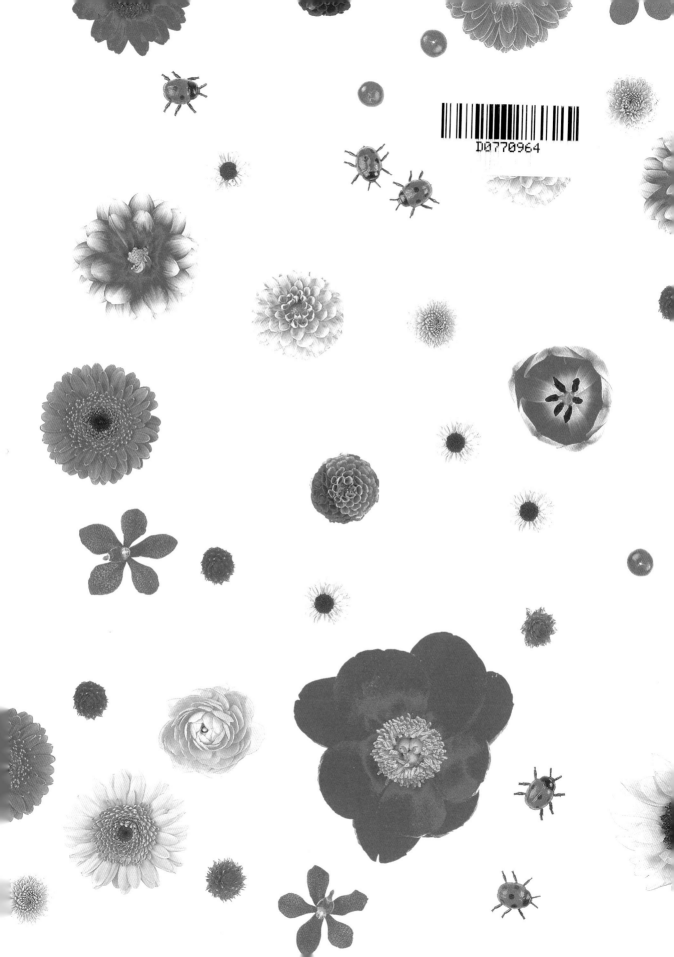

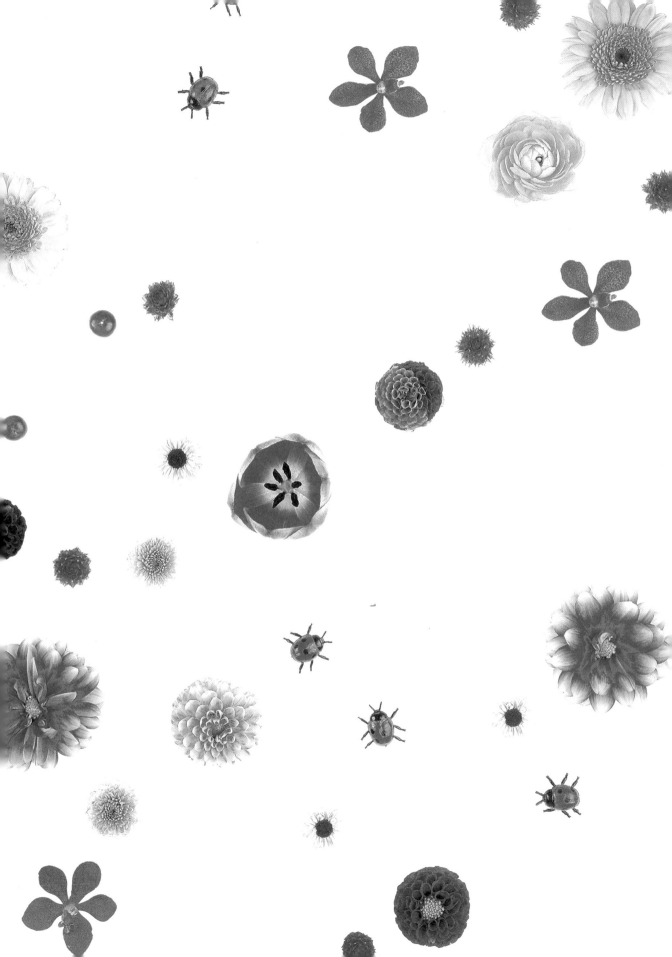

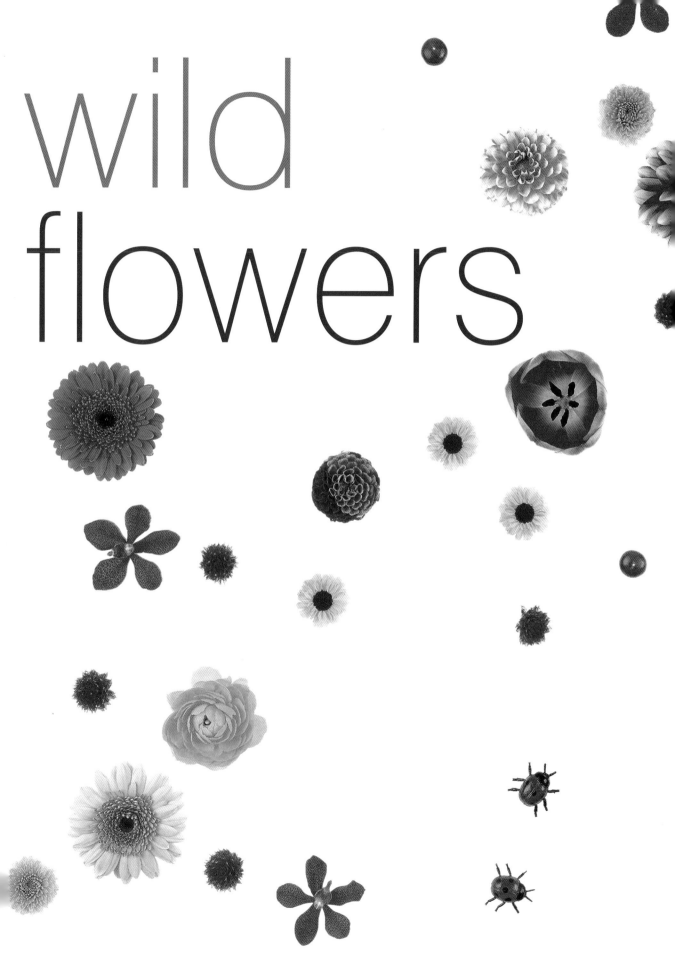

wild
flowers

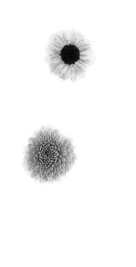

Wild

flowers

david stark
and avi adler

photographs
by
mick hales

Clarkson Potter/Publishers
New York

Published by Clarkson Potter/Publishers, New York, New York.
Member of the Crown Publishing Group, a division of Random House, Inc.
www.randomhouse.com

Clarkson N. Potter is a trademark and Potter and colophon are registered
trademarks of Random House, Inc.

Printed in Singapore

Design by 2x4, New York
Georgie Stout, Alice Chung, and Karen Hsu

Library of Congress Cataloging-in-Publication Data is available upon request.

ISBN 0-609-60938-6

10   9   8   7   6   5   4   3   2   1

First Edition

To David, who against all odds made this amazing book, and to my dad, who quietly and unknowingly embedded in me the love for flowers, gardening, and so much more.
—Avi

I made this as a gift for you, Avi, to celebrate all we've accomplished together, and for you, mom and dad—thank you for teaching me that I can do anything I set my mind to.
—David

begin with something
very simple...

or even ordinary

(and with a few hints)
make something…

incredible.

Imagine…

We fell into the floral realm by accident—two struggling artists looking for a way to support their painting. Ten years and countless roses (and thorns) later, we've found ourselves with a foot in both worlds—event planners who approach floral design like an art installation, and painters whose pigments are flowers and plants.

Of course—just like anyone—we are moved and inspired by flowers themselves: a hike along a wooded trail, a visit to a big-city botanical garden. But it's not that type of stimuli that spurs the designs that set us apart. For those creations we seek, and find, elsewhere. If we had to name the one quality that has allowed our design firm to flourish, it's the delight we take in finding inspiration in the most unlikely places, and our ability to create beauty with what others might deem ordinary or even tacky.

Take the lowly carnation, for instance. This inexpensive, sturdy flower comes in lots of colors, has gorgeous, ruffled petals, and makes a dense, vibrant arrangement. Yet despite these virtues, until recently if a florist even suggested using carnations, the client would utter a little gasp of horror: "Oooh noooo! I *hate* carnations!"

We, too, were once flower snobs, guilty as anyone of proliferating that attitude about carnations. Until, that is, we imagined a world where large, buoyant orbs of carnations adorned with bright, happy polka dots could float in an azure swimming pool like rubber duckies or roll across a summer lawn.

Baby's breath? We used to roll our eyes and explain, "It's not even in our vocabulary." Then we dreamed of suspending huge, fluffy clouds of baby's breath from the ceiling for a big party.

Mums? "So pedestrian." But have you ever seen a "wall" of fresh lemons floating in a sea of lemon yellow mums? A wall? Fabulous!

Somehow, most of us have been conditioned to think that to be really, really chic, you must avoid certain flowers at all costs—"tastes" as ingrained in supposed sophisticates as knowing which month to be in Gstaad.

We beg to differ: Carnations—in fact, all flowers—are intrinsically beautiful. It's only how these flowers are used that gives them a bad rap.

In our bustling New York event design firm, we've had the magical experience of seeing the studio filled with thousands of the most incredible, sumptuous, white peonies, big and fluffy as dollops of whipped cream.

A free-standing "wall," created for a party at the DIA Center for the Arts, is fashioned from eight thousand fresh lemons, thousands of chrysanthemums, and a whole lot of glue.

Guests at the Robin Hood Foundation's annual gala sip cocktails beneath a cloud-filled sky of baby's breath.

And we've worked with all kinds of amazing flowers—garden roses, orchids, lilies of the valley—exotic, rare, heirloom species flown in at great expense in the middle of winter from far-off lands.

Wild Flowers is not about that. It's about making cool stuff with flowers (some you're probably not used to working with) and looking at the regular world around you to find the inspiration and the materials to make these cool things. It may not be easy (and you may even want to resist!), but in the next many pages, we intend to help you unlearn all your flower prejudices. From transforming a common drinking glass into the most glam vase to creating a happy snowman out of, yes, carnations, we hope *Wild Flowers* will plant the notion that you can create many amazing things beyond bouquets with flowers, and you don't need your own greenhouse or a wholesale flower license to make them.

The garden is a great place for discovery (and yes, magic), but look further. Feather boas, children's toys, a walk through the hardware store, a trip to the greengrocer, a rummage through the attic, even gazing at the sky—inspiration and materials for making something fabulous are everywhere.

Our message in a bottle:

Dear Flower Lover,
Look at the world around you
and fall in love with flowers and things
that you've never looked at twice.

Be open to the everyday things—
they might bring the biggest inspiration of all!

Love,
David and Avi

if you look around,
you might find...

2 3 4 5 6 7 8 9 10 11 12

20 21

24 25

28 29

31 32 33 34 35

38 39 40 41

47 48

53 54 55

58 59 60 61 62

64 65 66 67

69 70 71 72

75 76 77

81 82 83 84

88 89

93 94 95 96 97

100 101 102 103

105 106 107

110 111 112 113 114

121 122

everyday things
that inspire.

feathers

carnations

holiday ornaments

stickers

Imagine…
an arrangement
with stickers

If the only thing that inspired your flower arrangements were flowers themselves, that would, we suppose, be fine. But the real kick we get from our
work is the inspiration we get from things other than flowers and plants.
Often, it's some seemingly forgettable, everyday object that really gets
us going.

Of course, since everyday objects are found in the places we visit every
day, you'll find these treasures in the most likely of places. One such trove
of inspiration is our local office supply store. Its merchandise-packed aisles
may not be as spectacular as the fields of sunflowers in Catalonia or the
tapestry of changing fall colors on a New England country road, but they
are bursting with great floral embellishments. A good example is (drumroll,
please!) stickers. That's right, those bright, pregummed dots, squares,
and rectangles meant for labeling office files that we use to create one-of-
a-kind floral containers and vases.

Don't let the word *vase* (rhymes with Oz) intimidate you. A vase is
anything that holds flowers: as elegant as Baccarat or as simple as a drinking glass. Choose what you like and make it your own special design by
embellishing it with stickers arranged in amazing patterns. Make dots into
polka dots, squares into checkerboards . . . after all, if you look beyond
the job they were pigeonholed to perform, you'll discover that stickers are
simply shapes waiting for you to arrange them.

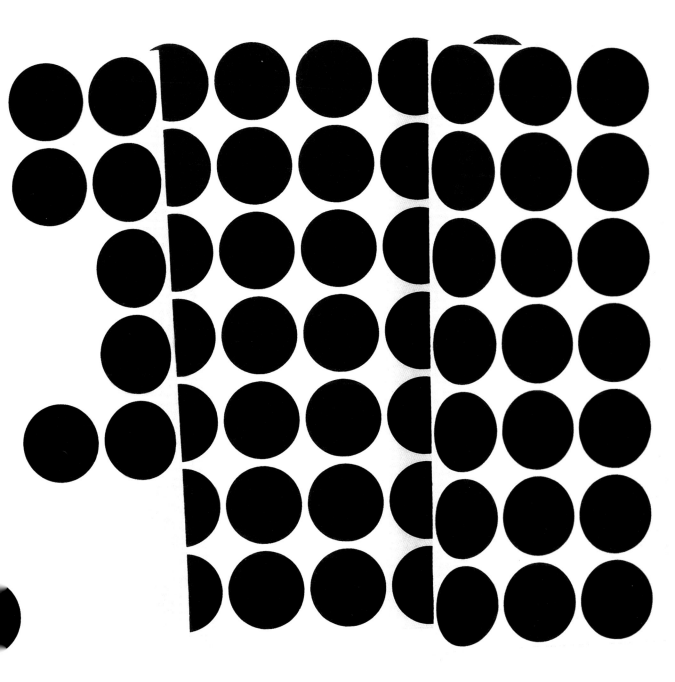

what you need

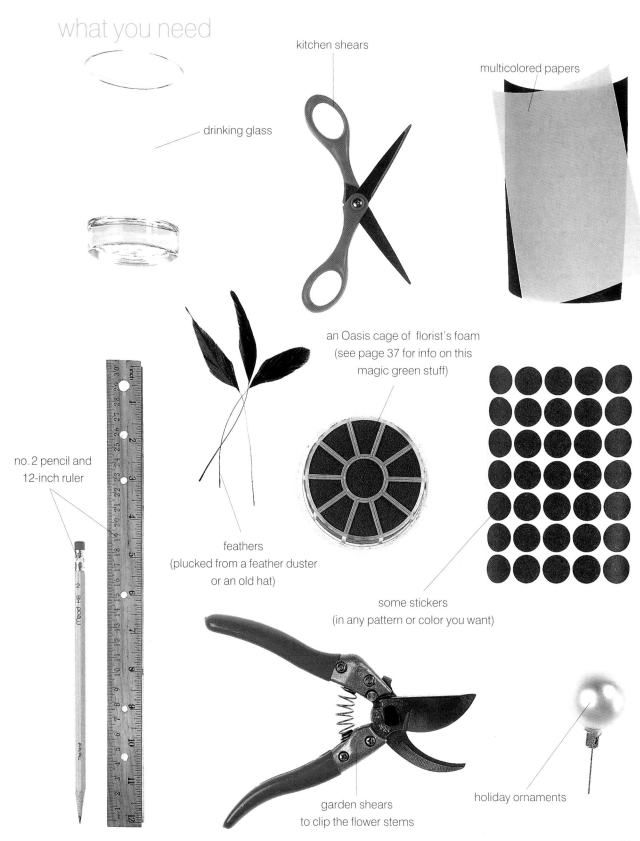

kitchen shears

multicolored papers

drinking glass

no. 2 pencil and
12-inch ruler

an Oasis cage of florist's foam
(see page 37 for info on this
magic green stuff)

feathers
(plucked from a feather duster
or an old hat)

some stickers
(in any pattern or color you want)

garden shears
to clip the flower stems

holiday ornaments

and some flowers
(carnations work
quite nicely!)

DIRECTIONS

1. To begin, put on some music to listen to while you work.

2. Find a glass container that you like. It can be a drinking glass or something that the world officially calls a vase. The important feature of this container, though, is that the diameter of its opening matches the diameter of the Oasis cage. (A little tip: It's much easier to work with a straight-sided container than one that is curvy.)

3. Starting at the very bottom of your container, place the stickers in any pattern that you want, moving all the way up and around the container until you reach the top.

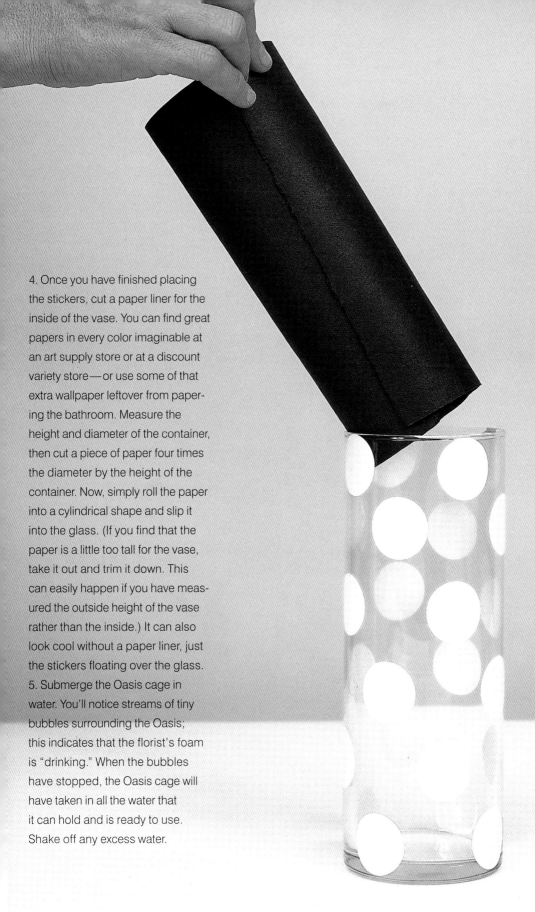

4. Once you have finished placing the stickers, cut a paper liner for the inside of the vase. You can find great papers in every color imaginable at an art supply store or at a discount variety store—or use some of that extra wallpaper leftover from papering the bathroom. Measure the height and diameter of the container, then cut a piece of paper four times the diameter by the height of the container. Now, simply roll the paper into a cylindrical shape and slip it into the glass. (If you find that the paper is a little too tall for the vase, take it out and trim it down. This can easily happen if you have measured the outside height of the vase rather than the inside.) It can also look cool without a paper liner, just the stickers floating over the glass.

5. Submerge the Oasis cage in water. You'll notice streams of tiny bubbles surrounding the Oasis; this indicates that the florist's foam is "drinking." When the bubbles have stopped, the Oasis cage will have taken in all the water that it can hold and is ready to use. Shake off any excess water.

6. Place the soaked Oasis cage on top of the vase. It will be supported by the rim of the container and eventually balanced by the flowers, so tape should not be necessary to hold the cage in place.

7. Make whatever flower arrangement you want, cutting each stem on an angle to about 2 inches in length. It doesn't matter whether you start at the top of the cage or on the sides as long as the flowers are inserted one next to the other with no space in between, ultimately hiding the edges of the Oasis. Another tip: Since the Oasis tends to leak while you work, it's neater to construct the arrangement using an empty glass as a stand-in for the actual sticker vase. After you are finished arranging the flowers, simply lift the Oasis cage out of the dummy vase, tilt it slightly to let any excess water drip out, and insert it into the top of the finished sticker vase.

8. After the finished arrangement is in place, you may feel that it still needs a little something. How about some jewelry or a hat? Don't hesitate to add some feathers, some glass Christmas balls, in fact any little adornments that you think will enhance the "outfit." Ask yourself, "What earrings should I wear with this dress?"

9. And have fun with it.
There are no rules.

Imagine...

an arrangement with sand stripes

It's happened countless times: You want to achieve a specific look, but can't find the right materials anywhere.

We often find ourselves in the exact same situation, but instead of feeling stumped in our quest for elegant answers we let our quandaries guide us to solutions we might otherwise never have discovered. The sticker vase, for example, began with an unsuccessful search for the perfect vase to complement a very glam black and white décor. Stickers satisfied only one portion of what we had in mind, though—we also really needed (okay, really badly wanted) stripes.

But where to find just the right stripes? The answer revealed itself one day as we were buying treats for our puppy at the corner pet store. There we experienced a floral epiphany: the aquarium sand and gravel in the store's fish tanks would make a really cool arrangement. They come in a wide array of stunning colors—from fluorescent blue to a deep chocolate brown—so the color combinations are endless. Just think how you could use them. Find that perfect sand to complement your wallpaper, your tablecloth, the sofa's upholstery, even your favorite shirt.

Sand is just the beginning, of course. Since there is no water inside your vase (ah, the wonders of Oasis!), you can fill your vase with anything that grabs your attention. Maybe you'll fill your vase with stripes of different flavored jelly beans. Maybe you'll opt for alternating layers of pennies and dimes, with a giant wad of greenbacks for your arrangement. Why not?

measuring cup

Oasis cage

drinking glass

black sand

white sand

34

. . . and more sand

and some flowers
(carnations are a good choice here, too)

DIRECTIONS

1. To begin, find a glass container that you like. It, too, can be a drinking glass or a "vase," and again, the important feature here is that the diameter of its opening matches the diameter of the Oasis cage.

2. Put some black sand into a measuring cup and pour as much of it as you want into the glass. Gently shake the glass to level it.

3. When the sand is level, add a layer of white sand on top. Gently shake the glass again.

4. Keep repeating these steps until you reach ½ inch from the top of your container.

5. Soak the Oasis cage in water until no more little fizzies are escaping and the foam is completely saturated. Shake off the excess water.

6. Place the soaked Oasis cage on top of the sand-filled container. It may be supported by the lip of the vase, or it may sit directly on the top level of sand.

7. Make whatever flower arrangement you want: perhaps a romantic bouquet of bright yellow roses cut from the garden or graphic mounds of white carnations dressed to the nines—then these arrangements become a great sidekick to their sticker pals. You may want to construct the actual arrangement using an empty glass as a stand-in for the actual sand container to avoid having the foam leak onto your sand stripes.

INSIDE THE OASIS CAGE

It's a floral designer's strongest ally: the Oasis cage, hidden keeper of freshness and form. Typically green and oh-so-handy, these mesh-covered blocks of florist's foam fit flowers into spaces no bigger than where you might put down your keys, purse, or yak (you know who you are).

The cages resemble miniature lobster traps, entirely filled with green foam (the Oasis), and they come in a variety of sizes. Buy them at craft stores (where they often come in pairs) or floral supply shops, or ask your florist to sell you a few.

Flower stems drink from the water-soaked foam (think sponge) just as if they were in a vase, replacing the need for a watertight container. The gridlike cage helps hold the arrangement in place and keeps the Oasis from breaking; the cage itself has a little lip beneath it that is designed to fit into the top of whatever you deem a "vase." We usually buy our cages, but sometimes make them ourselves, and you can, too. It's easy. You'll need:

- Oasis foam (it comes in bricks of varying sizes)
- chicken wire from the hardware or home supply store
- green floral tape from a floral supply or a craft store
- some kind of waterproof tray or dish (We often use plastic flowerpot saucers because they have good lips, don't leak, are inexpensive, and come in a gazillion sizes, from 4 to 26 inches in diameter.)

Cut the Oasis to fit the dish. Make it any shape you want—a tall cone to make a Christmas tree, maybe the shape of a house, or just a simple mound. Hold the chicken wire over your form, then cut the chicken wire to size, tailoring it neatly at the edge of the dish. Secure the chicken wire with floral tape to the dish by crisscrossing the tape over the top of the chicken wire and then back around under the dish in the opposite direction (like ribbon on a gift box).

Be sure that your flowers cover all edges and completely hide the cage.

Voilà!

Ivy

yes, they're real!

Imagine...
a flower painting

"You *can't* do that with flowers!" Oh, how often we've heard that mantra. It's not unusual for us to run into skeptics when we try to explain a new idea. We've found, though, that nothing turns a skeptic into a believer like seeing the idea come to life. And the ability to envision a design is the first step to making it real. Our background as painters has led to an ever-broadening palette of designs, such as flower paintings, that have met their share of nay-sayers. Those same skeptics, of course, are the first to cheer when they see it up on the wall. Yes, you *can* make a painting with flowers.

As with any painting, your canvas can be as big or as small as you want it to be. Want to make a triptych of 3-by-6-foot panels? Be our guest. But maybe you want to start on a more manageable scale.

First thing to remember: These are paintings made with fresh flowers, so they'll last only a couple of days. In order to extend their beauty, make them right before that special occasion, mist frequently, and hang in a cool place out of direct sunlight and away from heat.

Our friend Donna's grandmother always stored her fresh flowers in the refrigerator every night before bedtime because, she said, "I'm not there to see them while I'm sleeping. Why waste their limited time in the world?" It's the same for flower paintings. Store small paintings in the fridge at night or, better yet, until party time. Keep big paintings in an air-conditioned space until ready for hanging.

Of course the real question is, What do you paint? Know at the start that almost any display of flowers across a panel is bound to be pretty, so don't worry about making a mistake. Look at patterns, swirls, a favorite Mondrian, or a splatter and imitate it in your flower painting. Maybe you want something on the realistic side: That garden club benefit seems to be calling for a daisy portrait in carnations. Or perhaps you will choose simply to hang a series of paintings on the wall in a variety of different shapes and sizes, salon-style. Berets optional.

what you need

scissors to cut
the ribbon

1½-inch-wide grosgrain ribbon
in your favorite color

wire cutter

garden shears to
clip the flowers

shallow bowl to soak
the flowers in

bottle of
Crowning Glory

wooden canvas stretcher
in any size you want

handful
of straight pins

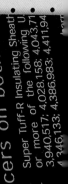

glue gun
and a glue stick

lots of 4-inch
pieces
of 19-gauge
straight wire

box cutter
to trim your foam

sheet of household
insulation foam
(enough to cover your frame)

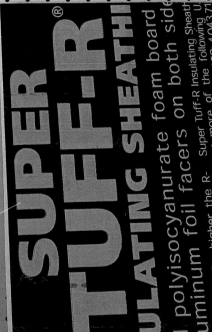

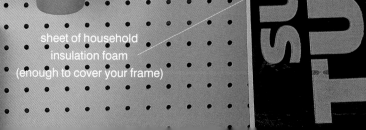
SUPER
TUFF-R®
ULATING SHEATHI

d polyisocyanurate foam board
uminum foil facers on both side
Super Tuff-R Insulating Sheathi
or more of the following: U.
3,940,517; 4,028,158; 4,043,7
3,940,517; 4,028,158; 4,411,94
⸺46,133; 4,386,983; 4,41
heat flow. The higher the R-
iulating power. Ask your sell-

lots of sweet gerbera daisies
(carnations, sunflowers, mums, and
roses also work really well)

To figure out how many flowers you need to make your painting,
it is helpful to have a calculator.
The formula is: (length) x (width) of your painting ÷ flower's diameter
For example, if your painting is 8 x 10 inches and your flower is
2 inches in diameter, the equation would be: 8 x 10 ÷ 2 = 40 flowers
So, you need approximately forty flowers to do the job, but you
should get a few extra just in case. . . .

THE GLORY OF CROWNING GLORY

The manufacturer calls it "a liquid shield for flowers and plants." We call it a godsend. Crowning Glory, made by the John Henry Company and available from floral supply stores or your florist, seals moisture inside a flower, extending its beauty far beyond its normal life. It also keeps dried flowers from shedding.

Crowning Glory preserves flowers in or out of water and is what makes flower balls and flower paintings possible. We also spritz arrangements in vases to add longevity to the bouquet. It's especially good for white flowers, which bruise more easily than colored flowers; the solution "toughens up" these little beauties and helps keep bruising to a minimum.

DIRECTIONS

1. Using your wood stretcher frame as a template, cut the foam to the outer dimensions of the stretcher.

2. Hot-glue the piece of foam to the front of the stretcher, holding it in place while it sets. A tip: If the "painting" is going to be on the larger side (more than 20 inches in any direction), we recommend reinforcing the glue with a couple of screws, screwing directly through the foam into the wood stretcher. A washer between the screw and the foam will prevent the screw from breaking through the foam.

3. Now it is time to prep your flowers. Remove the flower stems, clipping them off close to the head of the blossom as possible.

4. In the bowl, mix a solution of half Crowning Glory and half water (this solution will seal moisture inside of the flower, prolonging its life). Mix enough solution to fully submerge the clipped flower heads, front and back. Clip a bunch of flower heads (as many at a time that comfortably fit in your bowl). Once the fronts and backs of the flower heads have been doused (they need to be submerged for only a couple of seconds), remove them from the bowl, shake off the excess solution, and place the flowers on a kitchen towel until you are ready to use them.

5. Cut your straight wire into 4-inch lengths and then bend each piece in half to form bobby pin shapes.

6. Carefully insert a wire pin directly through the very center of the flower head from front to back, and gently slide it through until the top of the pin lies flush with the flower face. The whole piece will resemble a giant thumbtack.

7. Insert the flower pins into the foam as you would stick a thumbtack into a bulletin board. Arrange the flowers into any pattern as you go, slightly overlapping their petals so that you don't have gaps in between (and therefore cover all the foam). Do not overlap the petals so much that you cover their centers and lose the shape of the individual blossoms.

8. Once you've covered the entire surface of the foam with flowers, tilt it slightly to shake off any excess Crowning Glory solution. Use the grosgrain ribbon to finish the edge of the flower painting, pinning it directly to the edge of the foam.

A tip: Carnations also make brilliant flower paintings, but they don't like to be dunked in Crowning Glory. Instead, put the solution in a spray bottle and mist the blossoms upon completion of your "painting." Use the pinning method shown on page 120, which varies slightly from the one used for flat-faced flowers, such as gerberas or mums.

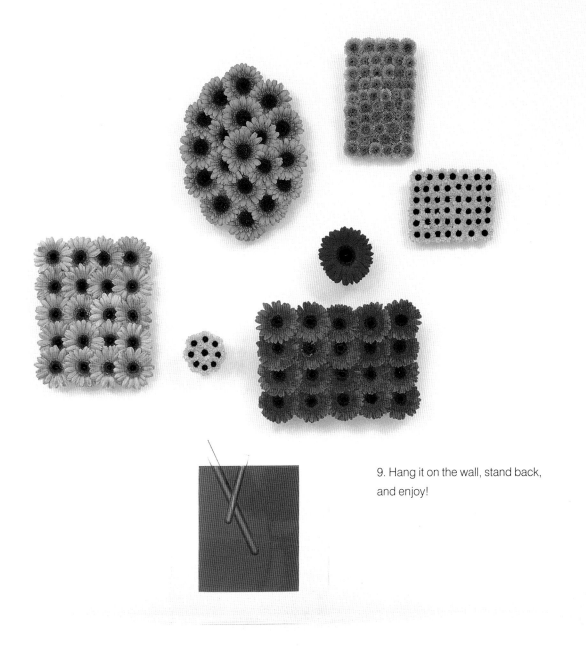

9. Hang it on the wall, stand back, and enjoy!

You can also make pictures with flowers.

Or patterns…

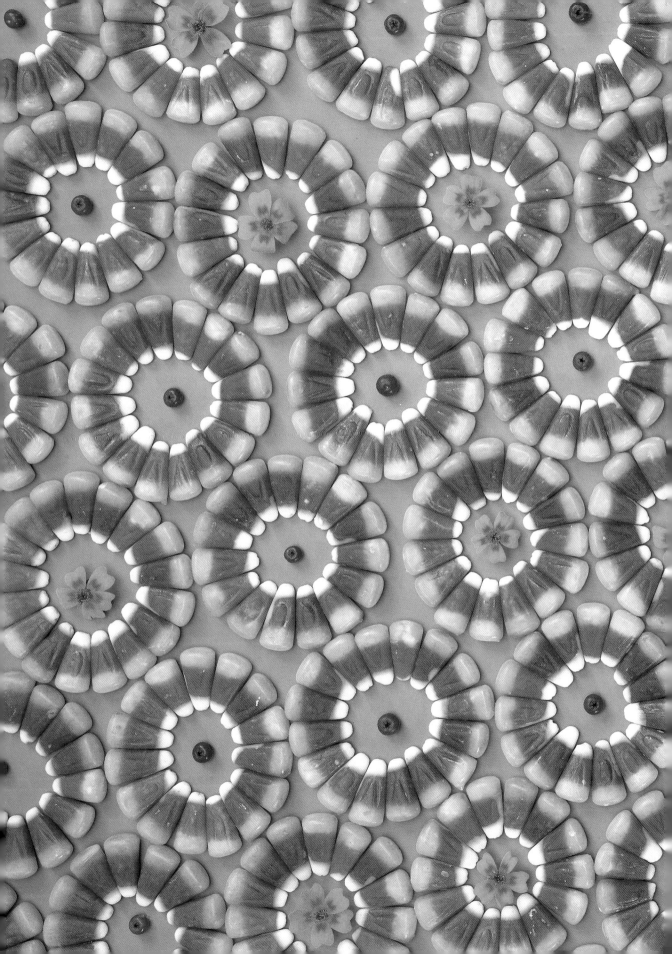

or balls.

child's ball

our ball

Imagine...
a flower ball

The first flower balls we ever made (and, as far as we know, the first flower balls *anyone* ever made) were for a very grand party—in fact, a ball—at the Whitney Museum of American Art in New York. When this crazy idea first came to us, it brought a little gleam to our eyes. "What if we made huge balls of white carnations?" we asked ourselves, knowing full well how taboo carnations were at that time. The challenge inspired us: Would it be possible to use a flower so long considered déclassé for an audience that was anything but?

Seventy thousand white carnations later, the answer was a decidedly triumphant yes. The guests, luminaries from fashion, design, art, business, and entertainment, were totally bowled over when they entered the transformed museum. The gallery walls were painted black to give the impression of an infinite space. From within this galaxy, huge, glowing, white orbs seemed to hover magically in midair.

That event started the flower ball rolling, and since then, we've had great fun making them with all kinds of blossoms for countless settings and occasions, grand to intimate. Try a flower ball as a centerpiece instead of a classic bouquet, placing it directly on the dining table. They look good as finials, too, on the first post of a stairway. For your summer barbecue, toss a bunch of balls in the pool with your blow-up toys. Tether them with fishing line and a clear plastic weight if you want to keep them in one general vicinity of the pool. Otherwise they'll tend to drift to the pool's edge (darned spinning of the Earth!).

what you need

bowl for soaking flowers
in Crowning Glory solution

Crowning Glory

lots of wire pins folded
from the straight wire

19-gauge straight wire cut
to about 5 inches

To figure out how many flowers are necessary to create your ball, you need to go back to your high school days of solid geometry. Remember when you grumbled, "When will I ever need to know this?" Well, now you do.
The formula is:

4 x 3.14 x the radius of your ball squared ÷ the diameter of your flower

Here's an example: You have a 5-inch diameter ball (which means a 2.5-inch radius) and you are using flowers that have a 2-inch diameter, so the equation is:

4 x 3.14 x 6.25 ÷ 2 = 39.25 flowers

It will take about thirty-nine flowers to do the job, but you should get a few extra just to be safe. In this case, we are covering an 8-inch diameter ball with sunflowers, which are about 3 inches in diameter. It took about seventy flowers to create this sphere (4 x 3.14 x 16 ÷ 3 = 66.98), and again, we always get extra just in case. . . .

gardening shears
for clipping flower stems

Styrofoam ball in any size
that you want (this is the thing that
makes it float)

lots of cute sunflowers
(dahlias, carnations, gerbera daisies,
mums, and roses also work well)

1. Begin by removing each flower's stem, clipping it off as close to the head of the blossom as possible.

2. Insert the wire pin directly through the very center of the flower face, and gently slide it through until the top of the pin lies flush with the flower face.

3. Once you've prepped your flowers, mix a solution of half Crowning Glory and half water in a bowl. Mix enough solution to fully submerge the flower heads, front and back. Once the front and backs of the flower heads have been doused (they need to be submerged for only a couple of seconds), remove them from the bowl, shake off the excess solution, and place the flowers on a kitchen towel until you are ready to use them.

4. Holding the blossom head carefully, insert its pin into the Styrofoam ball, and gently push on the head of the blossom until the flower is pressed flush against the Styrofoam.

5. Continue pinning flowers next to each other, slightly overlapping their petals, until you have covered the entire sphere. Take care to pin the flowers close enough to each flower so that there are no gaps between (and therefore the Styrofoam is totally covered), but don't overlap the flowers so much that you cover their centers and lose the shape of the individual blossoms.

A tip: Carnations (as seen on the preceding pages) are amazing flowers to use for flower balls. Not only are carnations very sturdy, but you can also make designs with them. Try polka dots, stripes, even letters and numbers. For the correct pinning method for carnations, look at page 120, and remember, carnations prefer to be misted with the solution, rather than submerged (this bruises the flower). After you've finished making an entire sphere, spray the whole ball with a misting bottle filled with the solution to seal in freshness.

Imagine...
an arrangement with seeds

When a sunflower matures, its face develops seeds (the same kind of seeds that you buy at the supermarket to feed the birds or to eat).

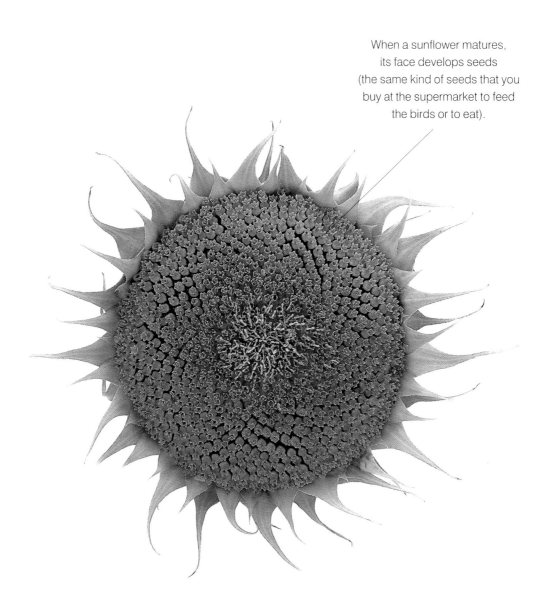

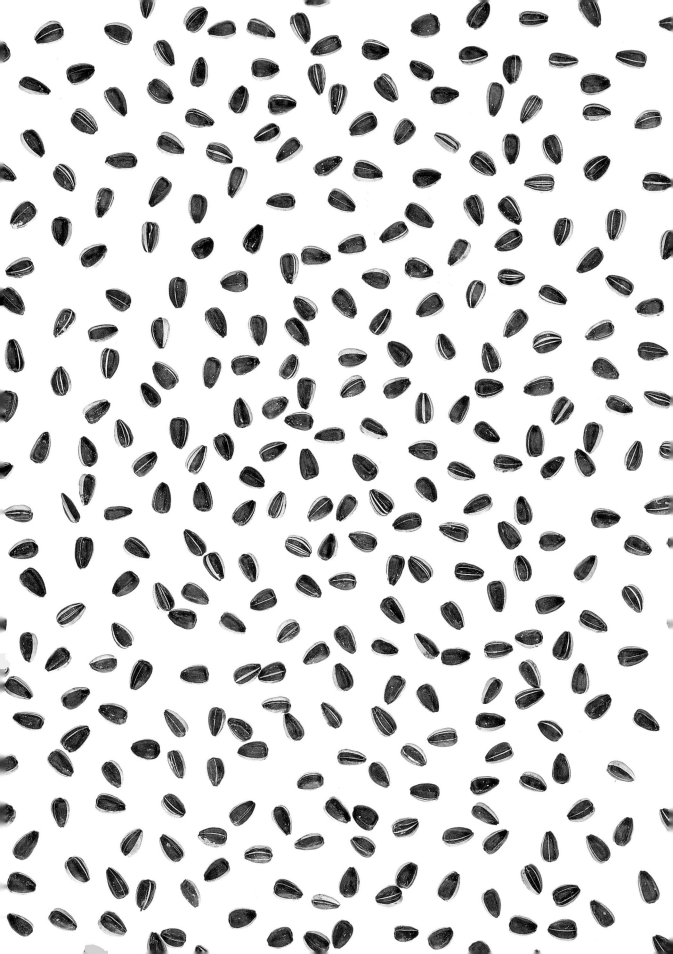

sunflowers

other little flowers

DIRECTIONS
1. Fill a vase with sunflower seeds and arrange a glorious bouquet of sunflowers (in an Oasis cage) on top.
2. Enjoy!

sunflower seeds

any old vase

When you are at the super-market picking up sunflower seeds, grab a bag of wheat berries, too. Find some contain-ers to fill with soil, and instead of sowing the seeds beneath the dirt, simply cover the entire surface of the soil with them.

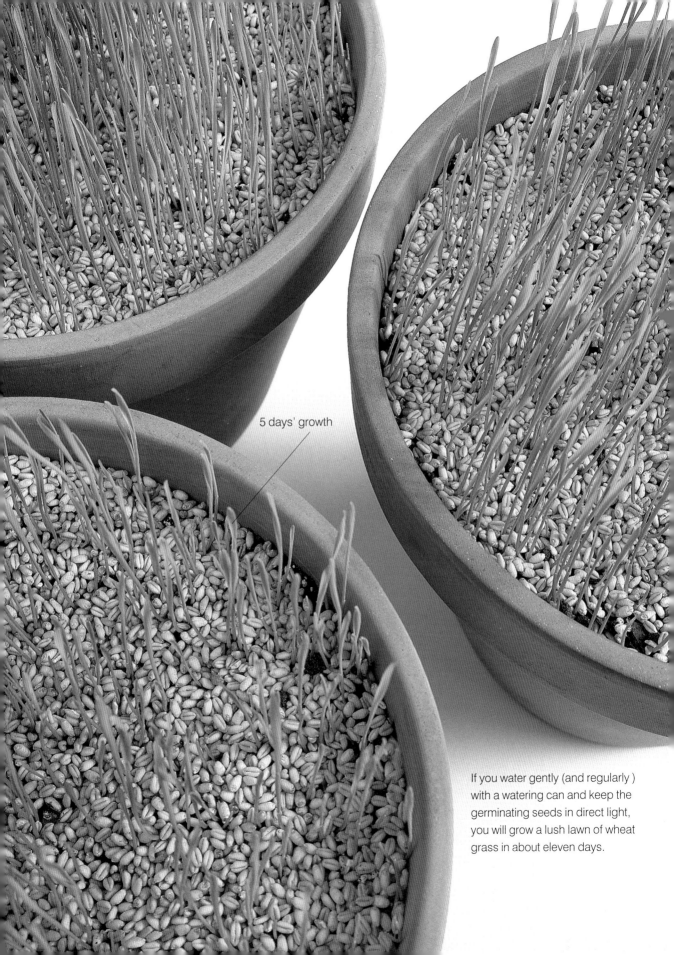

5 days' growth

If you water gently (and regularly) with a watering can and keep the germinating seeds in direct light, you will grow a lush lawn of wheat grass in about eleven days.

11 days' growth

Imagine...
an instant garden

You normally see flats of wheat grass at health bars, a miniature carpet of green lawn waiting to be clipped and transformed into an extremely healthy (if foul-tasting) elixir. These expanses of green have become something of a modern decorating cliché, the purist's "house plant" and the perfect complement to minimalist, modern interiors.

We, however, pursue a somewhat different approach (*quel surprise!*). We take that age-old, symbolic idea of "bringing the garden indoors" and make it real.

You can grow your own wheat grass, but heath food stores keep commercially grown wheat grass in stock for their juices (check with your florist, too), and many will let you buy flats from them. If you need several, order them in advance.

At 10 by 20 inches, grass flats lift easily out of the tray in one piece. Knowing the dimensions lets you quilt the flats together to create a lawn of any size. Your lawn may be 10 by 20 inches (just one flat), 20 by 40 inches (four flats), or whatever size you want—100 flats can make a lawn just over 8 by 16 feet!

Cut flats with a kitchen knife to make shapes. Lay a grass flat over a small, inverted bowl to create a "hill." Create "putting green" place mats for your next dinner party. Landscape your indoor garden around a "pond" you make from a shallow dish of water.

Remember, one of the nicest things a garden grows is inspiration.

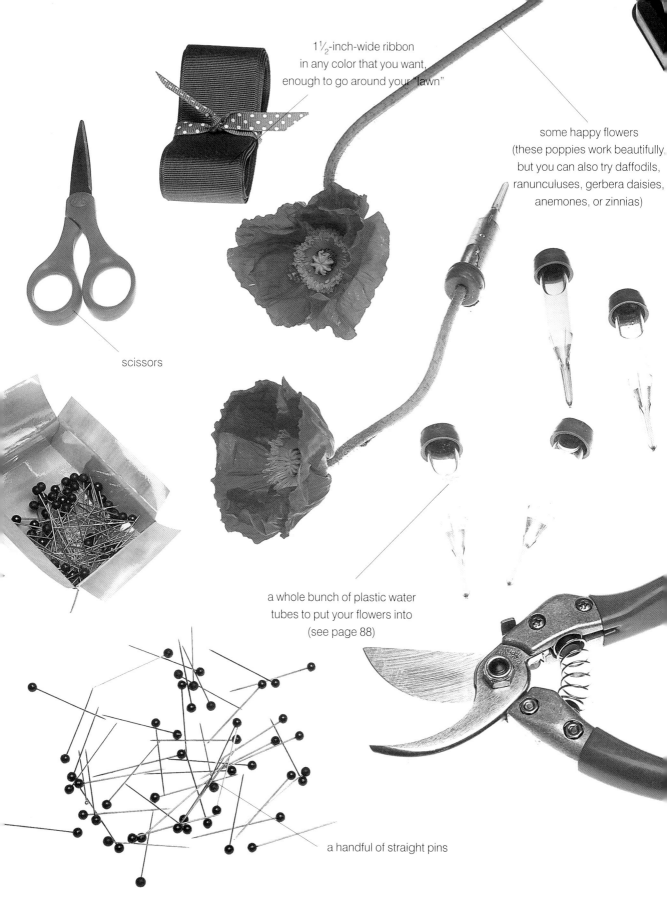

1½-inch-wide ribbon
in any color that you want,
enough to go around your "lawn"

some happy flowers
(these poppies work beautifully,
but you can also try daffodils,
ranunculuses, gerbera daisies,
anemones, or zinnias)

scissors

a whole bunch of plastic water
tubes to put your flowers into
(see page 88)

a handful of straight pins

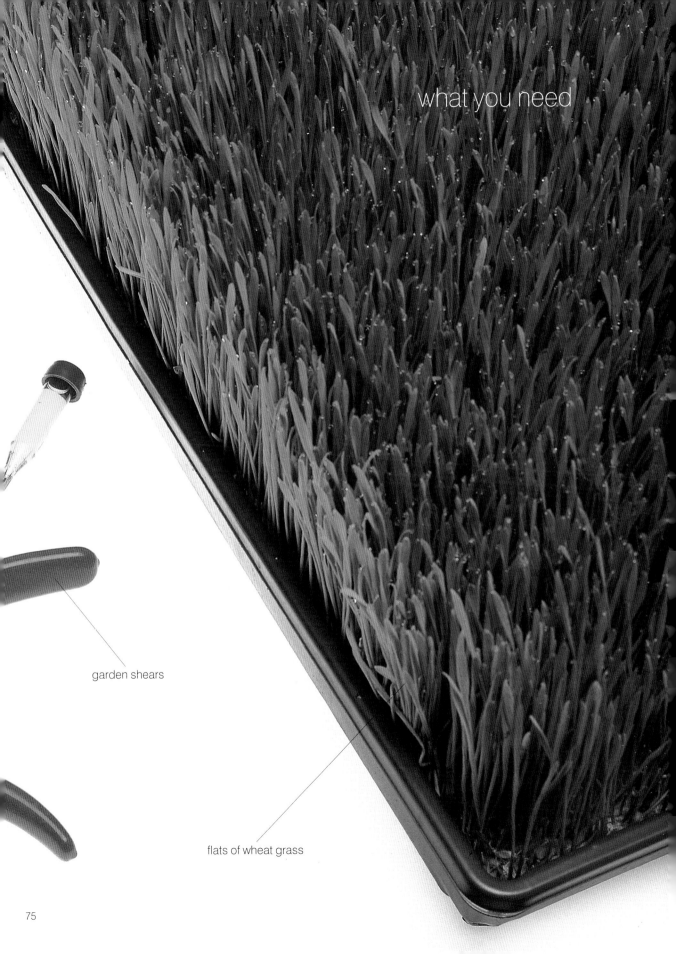

garden shears

flats of wheat grass

DIRECTIONS

1. Piece together flats of wheat grass to form a table-length patch of lawn.

2. Finish the edges of your lawn by pinning ribbon around the entire outer edge of your carpet of green.

3. After giving your flowers a fresh cut, insert their stems into filled water tubes.

4. "Plant" them in sweet groupings to create a garden table setting. . . .

inside...

or outside.

If only the results of outdoor gardening were instantaneous! For several years our large garden in upstate New York has been a wonderful, ongoing exercise in patience. Just when you think you've got it all figured out, something throws you for a loop. It rains only twice all summer, ravenous deer help themselves to the heirloom tulips before they've had a chance to say, "Hello, Spring!" or pesky Japanese beetles make mincemeat out of the roses. *Ah, wilderness!* indeed.

As event designers, we've worked with oodles of folks who have (with only the best intentions) tried to hold sway over Mother Nature, cajoling their gardens into blooming at the exact moment their daughter is to walk down the aisle amidst glorious flowers and plants in full bloom. Sometimes nature cooperates. Sometimes it doesn't. But why leave it to chance?

Say you wake up one bright summer day and feel like surprising your sweetheart with a picnic in a wildflower meadow. No wildflower meadow nearby? No problem. If you can't find the perfect spot, make one yourself.

Unlike bona fide gardening, you won't be constricted by such troublesome realities as soil and light conditions. And no need to wait ten years for your garden to mature and unfurl its vibrant flag of a million flowers exactly where and when you want. Just "plant" water-tubed flowers directly into an actual lawn.

Have fun. Mix flowers and colors. Make patterns. Spell your sweetie's name in flowers. Make it look like the garden has always been there. Whatever you choose, you'll definitely get Brownie points.

what you need

snacks of your choice

Chips

1 OZ.(28g)

a cold drink

a fresh apple

ODE TO A FLOWER TUBE

When exotic blossoms from tropical paradises arrive in America, they come with a little vial of water snuggled at the end of the stem. It's the same flower tube that keeps your honey's Valentine bouquet fresh in transit from the florist.

We like to think of flower tubes as tiny vases: Self-contained and filled with water, they let you put flowers anywhere.

Though available in bulk—usually in quantities of a thousand—you can probably get what you need from your florist. Choose Aquapics (or simply "water picks") large enough to hold the stem of your flowers with enough room to spare for water. Push the stem through the slit in the cap all the way to the bottom of the tube so it can drink every drop. Certain flowers drink faster than others (a rose can go through a tube of water in six hours while orchids can last up to four days), so don't forget to check on the kids and add fresh water when necessary.

Use tubes to put a single bloom or a minigarden anywhere that might like a flower—and that's practically everywhere:

- a "garnish" for your hors d'oeuvres tray
- a perfectly outrageous bonnet
- a stylin' dog collar for Frisky
- fresh flowers to enhance a holiday wreath, garland, Christmas tree, etc.
- when you can't fit another stem into a vase, but you want to add more flowers
- in nonwatertight containers (a cracked vase, say, or an ice cream cone)

lots of florist's plastic water tubes (Aquapics) filled with water

a whole lot of brightly hued zinnias
(also try gerbera daisies,
margaritas, and daffodils)

DIRECTIONS

1. Pack a yummy lunch and bring it to the perfect spot for a picnic. Choose a spot that is not too sunny— you and your flowers will appreciate it later. Once you've spread your blanket, start "planting" the "garden" around it.

3. Then push the tube into the ground as far as you can. It is best if the rubber top of the tube rests flush with the surface of the ground. This way it will be hidden by the surrounding grass, and the flower will look like it is growing naturally.

2. Begin with one flower. Give it a fresh cut and insert the stem into a filled water tube, pushing the stem in until it touches the bottom of the tube.

4. If you find that the ground is too hard to easily insert the flower tube into it, use a screwdriver to make a hole in the ground first. The flower tube will then slide right in.

5. Repeat tubing and planting the flowers as many times as you like until your garden is complete (or until you run out of flowers).

Bon appétit!

Imagine...
a flower cloud

It takes a great deal of trust (and vision) for a client to put faith in some of the wacky ideas that we come up with for parties—especially those with no real frame of reference, such as our ethereal concept of a fluffy, cloud-filled sky of baby's breath. So, hats off to our pals at the Robin Hood Foundation. This New York–based organization that effectively "takes from the rich and gives to the poor" gave us carte blanche to create a setting for their fundraising gala. Thanks to them, we fell in love with this underdog flower.

The inevitable pairing of baby's breath with its best friend, the red rose, is not a combo in our top ten but, in our search to make "clouds," a funny, wonderful thing happened: We looked at baby's breath without its usual partner in crime and realized it's quite beautiful. Still, we didn't need any great love of baby's breath to inspire us. It was our fascination with the great, white, cotton-ball puffs in the sky.

Of course, making a sky full of clouds is a grand gesture, but we've found that the flower works beautifully in more intimate settings as well. Maybe you'll lasso a baby's breath cloud for an elegant table décor of delicate wisps—perfect for a dinner for two.

Sometimes the easiest way to create something new is to find inspiration in things that have been there all along. That's what happened with baby's breath—we opened our minds, dropped our preconceived notions of what passes for chic, and rediscovered a flower that, we now realize, is surprisingly highbrow. We made clouds by coming down to earth.

Who knew?

Imagine...
an arrangement
with drinks

Sometimes beauty resides in the most unexpected places. Consider the dizzying display of liquid refreshments found in convenience store coolers. A bottle of orange soda, for instance, may never have struck you as a real dazzler, but with light streaming through it, illuminating the liquid like stained glass, we find the color as vivid and full of possibilities as a box of oil paints. For vases of stunning luminosity and crystalline hues, we don't turn to a master glass blower. We simply fill a clear glass with, say, Gatorade.

Using soft drinks as coloring did not occur to us immediately. Like so many endeavors, it was the result of lengthy research—and a bit of kismet. First we tinted water with food coloring. It worked okay, but the subtlety of the colors was, well, too subtle. And the food coloring stained our glassware. We tested all kinds of solutions of watered-down inks and fabric dyes. That worked better, but it was messy and expensive.

Then one day, while shopping in the local supermarket, we noticed the almost eerie beauty of a shaft of light piercing a bottle of Gatorade. Suddenly, it came to us: the perfect way to satisfy our desire for a luminous blue vase. Now we could finally create that all-blue party that had eluded us as well as a whole spectrum of other party color palettes by merely sampling the vast rainbow of drinks on the market.

Maybe you'd like to create the color wheel in a circle of clear vases or arrange variously colored water vases in front of a window for something akin to cathedral style.

For a friend's holiday party, we illuminated several liquid vignettes with a scattering of candles—no flowers at all. Our pal gushed to everyone, "Did you see my colored water *tableaus*!" To this day, this trendsetter has no idea that his fancy party décor came from his own refrigerator.

One caveat: Throw away the empty bottles before guests arrive! As a wise mother once said, "No one needs to know all your secrets all the time."

baby's breath

marabou boa

Gatorade

what you need

some brightly colored drinks to fill
an array of glassware of your choice

DIRECTIONS
1. Find a whole bunch of glass
containers. They can be all
different sizes and shapes—
whatever you love (or whatever
is in your cupboard).
2. Fill the glassware with drinks of
your choice and scatter candles all
around to illuminate the tableau.

It's very beautiful without flowers.

...it's also very beautiful with flowers.

3. To add flowers to the mix, soak an Oasis cage in water until no more bubbles seep out. Shake off the excess water and sit the cage on the lip of the glass. Give your flowers a fresh cut, inserting the stems into the florist's foam tightly enough that you can no longer see the Oasis. To hide the edges of the Oasis cage, we add a gossamer collar of marabou boa, pinned directly into the Oasis. This boa is not a necessity (you can use the flowers to hide the Oasis). We just happen to love the ephemeral quality of the downy frill.

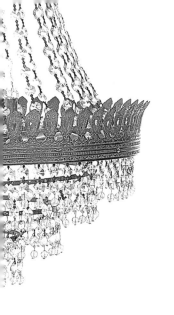

Why not serve your guests cocktails that match, too?

Imagine...
painted pots

If someone were to accuse us of being too in love with color, we'd have to admit: guilty as charged. It's much more than just trying to find the perfect color of flowers, though; we want our vases to be just right, too.

Our painters' backgrounds often come in handy when we're searching for that vase of a particular color. And we *always* want a particular (read: specific, hard-to-find) color. When we have to, we simply paint our vase the perfect hue.

Common terra-cotta pots take paint perfectly. We usually use flat (not glossy) housepaint, but we also like art and poster paints. Whichever you use, a rich, velvety finish normally requires a couple of coats.

Remember that terra-cotta pots have a drainage hole in the bottom, so they need a watertight liner. Use a smaller vase, drinking glass, plastic container, paper cup, or whatever holds water and can be hidden inside the pot. Of course, it's not just pots that look good painted. Add your own color to a teakettle, toy boat, wine bottle, wooden shoe, Orangina bottle, the kitchen sink—anything that can serve as a vase.

That's right: Everything *and* the kitchen sink!

It may be the color of your flowers that
inspires the color of your vase.

Or perhaps it's the color of
your tablecloth.

Or maybe it's the colors of
the season that inspire.

Imagine...
a flower snowman

We've developed a bit of a snowman fetish. Every year around the holidays, our staff is reduced to a bunch of giggling kids, cooing "They're sooooo cuuuuute!" at the legion of snowpeople that take over the studio. It's funny how things evolve. We never had any particular interest in snowmen until we started making carnation balls. We made this conceptual leap when we were asked to create the décor for a "Winter Wonderland" holiday party. Only then did it occur to us to take three flower balls and stack 'em.

That's really the essence of this book: Make the visual connection and take the conceptual leap. Use our ideas and techniques to make other fab things. A snowman easily becomes a snowwoman if you add two little snow breasts! String together several balls to make a deliciously colorful caterpillar. Alternate "stripes" to make a flower beach ball. Use orange carnations to turn a flower ball into a pumpkin. Add burgundy carnations to "carve" out eyes, a nose, and a mouth to make a jack-o'-lantern.

But don't stop there. Cinderella's godmother turned a pumpkin into a carriage. What will you turn it into?

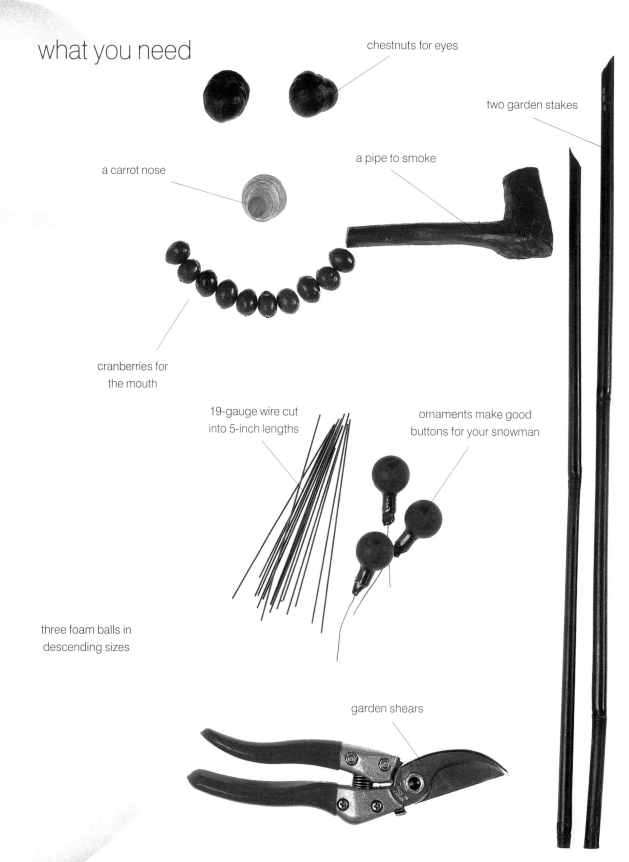

what you need

chestnuts for eyes

two garden stakes

a pipe to smoke

a carrot nose

cranberries for
the mouth

19-gauge wire cut
into 5-inch lengths

ornaments make good
buttons for your snowman

three foam balls in
descending sizes

garden shears

and lots and lots of white carnations
(to figure out how many flowers you need,
see the formula on page 61)

1. To begin, cut the entire stem off each blossom, and thread the wire directly through the base, bending the wire so as to form a bobby pin shape.

2. Insert the wired carnations directly into the largest Styrofoam ball so that the base of the carnation kisses the surface of the Styrofoam. Continue adding carnations, one right next to the other, carpeting the ball densely with blossoms until you are about halfway finished.

3. At this point, use a kitchen knife to cut a little slice off the unfinished side of the Styrofoam ball. Turn the ball over, and sit the newly flat side of the ball on a dessert plate or in a shallow dish.

4. Once you've stabilized the ball, pierce the top of the ball with the two garden stakes, making sure you sink them vertically into the ball about halfway in and 1 to 2 inches apart. This will form the armature for the next ball to be threaded onto. Cut the protruding stakes so that when a new ball is threaded onto it, it too, will go about halfway into the ball. Now continue adding carnations around the protruding stakes until the ball is completely covered.

5. Carpet the second largest ball completely with flowers, then center it over the garden stakes, pressing it down until it touches the larger ball. Insert two more garden stakes into the top of this ball in the same manner, preparing an armature for the snowman's head.

6. Repeat this process with the third ball, threading it onto the garden stakes upon completion.

7. Then have fun. Add whatever features or fashions you so desire: hat, scarf, nose, eyes, mouth, buttons, bra—go wild!

I didn't do it!

ACKNOWLEDGMENTS

We could not have made this book without the support, help, and talents of many people—thank you:

Carla Glasser, our agent, for believing in our vision and making sure that it would be realized just the way we wanted it to be; Pam Krauss, our editor, for *her* vision and embrace; Georgie Stout of 2 x 4 who, with Alice Chung and Karen Hsu, helped conceive *Wild Flowers,* making it look and feel so special; Mick Hales for his unwavering patience and for capturing the hyper-real world of our minds on film so beautifully; John Morse, who is an incredible "security blanket"; Susie Montagna, who worked alongside us planning and creating every visual that went into this book, and others who made this book pop; Sylvia Weinstock for her fabulous polka dot cake; our great pal Lolo, for lending her sexy legs; Bernardaud for all of their exquisite china; Cristal Saint Louis and William Yeoward for their amazing stemware; Baker Furniture for their fabulous mirror; and Regula's Specialty Cakes of Brooklyn, who made us the yummy treats in our holiday spread. And a final, special thanks to the entire cast of our little design collective called Avi Adler, who helped conceive and perfect all of the ideas that found their way into this book. In particular, thank you, Susie, Josh, Ariane, Roy, Charo, Sheila, Marco, Harry, Gary, Natie, Maria, and everyone else who has worked so hard with us over the years—bouquets all around!